MW01255012

UNCOMMON
REVOLUTIONARY

A Creative Minds Biography

UNCOMMON REVOLUTIONARY

A Story about Thomas Paine

by Laura Waxman

illustrations by Craig Orback

Carolrhoda Books, Inc./Minneapolis

For Shaan, an uncommon human being —LW

*The illustrator would like to thank Bryan Woolley
who modeled for the paintings as Thomas Paine
and helped with photography. —CO*

Text copyright © 2004 by Carolrhoda Books, Inc.
Illustrations © 2004 by Craig Orbeck

Carolrhoda Books, Inc.
A division of Lerner Publishing Group
241 First Avenue North
Minneapolis, MN 55401 U.S.A.

Website address: www.lernerbooks.com

Library of Congress Cataloging-in-Publication Data

Waxman, Laura Hamilton.
    An uncommon revolutionary : a story about Thomas Paine / by Laura
Hamilton Waxman ; illustrations by Craig Orback.
        p.   cm. — (A creative minds biography)
    Summary: Introduces Thomas Paine, whose interest in politics and
adventure led him from England to the American colonies where the
articles and pamphlets he wrote helped generate support for the
Revolution.
    Includes bibliographical references and index.
    ISBN: 1–57505–180–X (lib. bdg. : alk. paper)
    1. Paine, Thomas, 1737–1809—Juvenile literature. 2. Political
scientists—United States—Biography—Juvenile literature.
3. Revolutionaries—United States—Biography—Juvenile literature.
[1. Paine, Thomas, 1737–1809. 2. Political scientists. 3. Revolutionaries.]
I. Orback, Craig, ill. II. Title. III. Series.
JC178.V5 W39 2004
320.51'092—dc21   2002152917

Manufactured in the United States of America
1 2 3 4 5 6 – DP – 09 08 07 06 05 04

Table of Contents

1

Boyhood in Britain

Eleven-year-old Thomas Paine leaned forward in his seat to hear every word his teacher said. Every inch of his body was tense and listening. Reverend William Knowles wasn't giving a lecture about mathematics or grammar. He wasn't even talking about poetry or the sciences, Tom's favorite subjects. Instead Reverend Knowles was spinning another tale about his youthful adventures on the high seas. Tom could almost picture himself there with his teacher, looking over the ship's deck and seeing nothing but endless water.

Tom knew where he would go if he were a sailor.

At school he had read a book about the British colony of Virginia. Since then he'd wanted to visit the American colonies. He wondered what life was like for the men and women who had bravely left Great Britain to live in the New World.

Like most British people at that time, Tom could only dream about such travels. Since his birth on January 29, 1737, Tom had never left his little town of Thetford, England. He was lucky that he could learn about other places, though. Many British people were unable to read. The British government did not pay for a child's schooling. Only the country's wealthiest citizens could afford a high-quality education. Tom's own parents had been forced to borrow money from a relative to pay for basic schooling for their son.

Tom's father, Joseph, earned a modest living as a staymaker. He made corsets for ladies to wear under their dresses. The business didn't make Tom's family rich, but it brought in enough to live simply. The Paines lived in a small brick cottage with a thatched roof. Their home sat at the top of Bridge Street in a modest part of town.

From an early age, Tom knew that something was different about his family. Most British men and women married people who practiced the same religion. But Tom's father was a Quaker while his mother, Frances Cocke, was an Anglican. The Anglican religion had become the Church of England, Britain's official religion. The Anglican services Tom attended were formal and traditional. In comparison, simplicity marked the Quaker services he went to with his father. Quakers had no ministers or leaders. They strived for equality and questioned more traditional religions.

To be raised by parents who practiced two different religions was almost unheard of in Britain. But it wasn't a problem for Tom. His parents may have gone to different churches, but they taught their son the same values. Be fair in your dealings with people. Stand up for what you believe in.

Tom learned different kinds of lessons on the streets of Thetford. The small, bustling market town had a population of about two thousand people. On market days, Thetford filled up with people from the surrounding villages. They came to buy products from local craftspeople such as Tom's father. But market day was nothing compared to the one time each year when the local jail executed its criminals. Tom always knew when this time of year had arrived because the town was overtaken by crowds of people who had come to watch.

A criminal's death sentence depended more on a person's position in the community than on the crime committed. A servant might well be hanged for stealing a bit of tea or sugar from her master's home. But a rich person would likely go unpunished for his crime—even for murder. After all, the rich ran the courts, made the laws, and received favors from the king. Most British citizens may have known that this was unfair, but they also knew that there wasn't much they could do about it. The poor would always be poor and powerless, and the rich would always be rich and powerful.

When Tom turned twelve, he had a lot less time to spend wandering around Thetford. That year he left school to begin working as his father's apprentice. As an apprentice, Tom was trained in the painstaking craft of making corsets. Eventually he would take over the family business. He knew this was a perfectly acceptable future. Plenty of boys learned their father's trade. And it wasn't as if he wanted to stay in school forever. But making corsets didn't seem very exciting or important.

Soon Tom's days were filled with endless hours of cutting and sewing cloth and weaving whalebone through rows of stitches. As his hands fumbled with the cloth, thread, and bone, Tom's mind would wander. Every so often he thought of his teacher's stories of adventure. Tom would probably never be able to leave Britain, much less Thetford. But surely it couldn't hurt to dream.

2

Adventure at Last

Tom had been a faithful apprentice for nearly seven years when an advertisement in the *Daily Advertiser* caught his eye. It requested the service of "Gentleman Soldiers and able-bodied Landmen." British captain William Death needed young, healthy men to serve as ship hands on the British warship the *Terrible.* The ship was to dock in London to accept new crew members. It would then set out to sea to fight the French, who were at war with Great Britain.

Being a staymaker didn't excite Tom any more at age nineteen than it had when he was a schoolboy. He was tired of watching his life drift by while he made corset after corset. He had to find a way to get on that ship.

Joseph Paine would never give his son permission to leave the shop and become a sailor. It was too dangerous. But Tom was determined. He snuck out of Thetford and made the journey to London. On a brisk November morning in 1756, he arrived at Execution Dock on the Thames River. He was ready to test his fate, just like Reverend Knowles had done.

As Tom waited with the other eager young men hoping to board the ship, he saw a man stomping angrily toward him. It took Tom a minute to believe his eyes. But, yes, that was definitely his father coming his way. And he looked very determined.

Joseph Paine had managed to track down his son. And he was kindly but firmly telling Tom he mustn't go. Something in his father's voice convinced Tom to forgo his plans for adventure. Instead, he agreed to stay in Britain and continue working as a staymaker. At least he didn't have to go back to Thetford. Joseph gave Tom permission to stay in London, as long as he could find a job.

Tom quickly found work as an assistant to Mr. John Morris, a staymaker on Hanover Street. Tom worked long hours in Mr. Morris's shop, but he still squeezed in time to explore his new home. London was noisy.

It was also smelly, overcrowded—and the most exciting place Tom had ever seen. The city had six theaters, a variety of bookshops, and more taverns and coffeehouses than he could count.

Unfortunately, being a staymaker was as dull as ever. Tom quit his job with Mr. Morris as soon as he learned that another ship was looking for men. This time, when the ship set sail on January 17, 1757, Tom made sure he was on it.

Tom's ship was called the *King of Prussia.* He quickly learned that life as a sailor was hard and dangerous. The captain and his crew earned their living by attacking French ships and stealing their cargo. They risked their lives each time they attempted an attack. At the same time, they had to avoid being attacked by other ships. In addition, rats, diseases, and seasickness plagued them. It was not, Tom decided, a good life for him. Six months was plenty of time at sea.

When Tom set foot on land on August 20, he had many stories to tell and enough money saved to pay for his lodgings in London. But most important, he had proved to himself that he could take control of his life.

Rather than look for work as a staymaker, Tom chose to live on the money he had earned as a sailor.

He wanted to take advantage of all that London had to offer. He spent hours skimming the pages of books in London's bookshops and chatting with people in coffeehouses and taverns.

Tom also went to public lectures offered by scientists Benjamin Martin and James Ferguson. The men spoke on topics such as geography, physics, mathematics, and astronomy. At these lectures, Tom was surrounded by men and women much like himself. They were shopkeepers, tailors, blacksmiths, and staymakers. They believed that all people should have the chance to improve themselves with knowledge. Learning shouldn't be reserved for the wealthy citizens of Britain, they said. Tom agreed. He loved having the chance to expand his mind.

While Tom's mind expanded, his savings shrunk. London was an expensive city. After several months, his money ran out. He had to face the dreary fact that he needed to find work once again. Being a staymaker seemed to be his only choice, but Tom wasn't interested in working for someone else. Since his adventure at sea, he had gotten used to being in charge of his own life. With some advice from Mr. Morris, Tom decided to set up his own shop in a small town called Sandwich. By the spring of 1759, he had settled into 20 New Street in Sandwich and set up shop.

At the age of twenty-two, he was finally working for himself.

Tom missed London, with its packed bookshops and coffeehouses and its fascinating scientific lectures. But slowly he became involved in his new home. He got to know the people in Sandwich through his work and through the Methodist church he had begun to attend.

Tom liked his new friends in Sandwich, especially Mary Lambert. She was a maid for a family in town. Mary was pretty and kind, and she seemed to like Tom. He began courting her, and by late summer they were engaged to be married. After their wedding day on September 27, 1759, the couple moved into a new home in Sandwich.

Tom learned that supporting two people was much harder than supporting one. On his own, he had been content to live simply and spend as little money as possible. Mary didn't expect a lot either, but she was another person to care for. Tom did what he could to gather enough work to support them both. But he was better at understanding scientific principles than he was at knowing how to run a business. Within months of his wedding day, his business in Sandwich failed. He was forced to sell off nearly everything he had to pay his debts, but he still owed money.

He and Mary packed up their few belongings and left town. Tom hoped to start another staymaking shop in the seaside town of Margate.

While Tom looked into opening a staymaker's shop, Mary prepared their new home. But things didn't go well. Soon after the move, Mary became ill and died.

Tom's friends and neighbors must have wondered how he felt about his wife's death. But Tom was a private person and didn't like to speak about the matter. There was no point in wallowing in self-pity, he said. Life would go on, and he would make the best of it.

3

Political Tax Collector

Penniless and on his own, Tom took a hard look at his life. He was simply no good at being a businessman. But what else could he do? He was the son of a humble staymaker, and he had little education to boast of. He knew that people of his class could choose from only a limited number of careers.

Tom did have one idea. He remembered hearing Mary talk about her father's work. James Lambert had been an exciseman. He had collected taxes on goods that came into Britain from foreign countries. That kind of work wouldn't make Tom rich, and it certainly wasn't a well-respected job. But it would provide a regular income. And best of all, it wouldn't involve the tedious work of sewing ladies' corsets.

Tom soon learned that applying for work with the Board of Excise Commissioners was not easy. Among other things, he needed several letters of recommendation, good handwriting, and a clean bill of health. Luckily, the board deemed Tom and his paperwork satisfactory. In December 1762, he learned that he would start out as a low-ranking exciseman in Grantham in the county of Lincolnshire.

Tom worked for more than a year visiting the region's innkeepers and merchants. He traveled on horseback to collect taxes on foreign goods such as coffee, tea, tobacco, and alcohol. In 1764 he was promoted to a more important position in the small town of Alford. Just five miles from the coast, Alford was a popular town for smugglers. These smugglers tried to sneak in goods from foreign ships. Then they could sell their goods secretly to local business owners without having to pay taxes. As part of his job, Tom rode his horse along the wet and windy roads of Alford's coast patrolling the area for smugglers.

Tom enjoyed his work but soon experienced a stroke of bad luck. In the summer of 1765, his supervisor accused him of writing false reports. The crime was called stamping.

Many excisemen committed this crime to avoid making enemies of local business owners and perhaps earn a bit of extra money for themselves. Excisemen were unpopular with business owners. After all, who wanted to pay taxes? Instead of visiting merchants and innkeepers to collect taxes, some excisemen wrote false reports. These reports told the British government that taxes had been collected when they really hadn't. Often a business owner would pay an exciseman a small bribe for writing these false reports. No one knows for sure if Tom actually committed this crime, but he lost his job because of it.

With the hope that he would be given another chance, Tom decided to reapply for a job with the Board of Excise Commissioners. In the meantime, he took odd jobs in London. In February 1768, he was offered a new post in the lively town of Lewes.

Tom quickly found housing with a local businessman named Samuel Ollive. Tom's landlord lived with his family above the tobacco shop he owned. He was also involved in local government. Samuel was always on the lookout for intelligent, energetic men to help make decisions about local politics. He encouraged Tom to get involved in the running of the city.

Tom soon became part of a group of men called the Society of Twelve. This group met twice each year.

They made important decisions for the town. They elected the town's various city officials. The society also organized people to collect the garbage and oversee the town's market. They even chose people to act as dogcatchers.

Tom's days as a struggling staymaker seemed far away. Being involved in local politics made him feel important. He had long ago learned how to take charge of his life. In Lewes he was helping to take charge of the town in which he lived. Instead of leaving everything up to King George III and Parliament, the people of Lewes had found a way to solve their own problems.

As much as Tom enjoyed being in the Society of Twelve, nothing gave him as much pleasure as the evenings he spent at the White Hart Inn. Once a week, the townsmen of Lewes got together there for drinks, oysters, and talk. They debated politics and just about everything else.

Tom found that he enjoyed speaking out on many topics. And he was good at it. People listened to the clever newcomer with dark, fiery eyes and thick brown hair. Tom had a way of making complex arguments easy to understand. He won more of the evening debates than anyone else at the White Hart. After a while, he became known as one the best debaters in town.

That gave him the confidence to write some clever poems and stories for the amusement of his friends.

Tom had been in Lewes for just over a year when his landlord and friend, Samuel Ollive, died. Samuel's wife, Esther, and Tom decided to run the shop together. They would sell both groceries and tobacco. That way Tom could help Mrs. Ollive earn an income, and he could supplement his measly earnings as an exciseman. Working with Mrs. Ollive also gave Tom an excuse to see more of the Ollives's daughter, Elizabeth. Tom had taken a liking to the smart, attractive twenty-year-old. Over the next months, they got to know each other better. By April 1771, they were married.

Tom hardly had time to enjoy life as a newly married man. His meetings and his two jobs kept him busy. And lately he had become involved in a debate among his fellow excisemen. The excisemen were angry about their pay. At meetings they grumbled among themselves. Only the king's Parliament had the power to raise their meager salaries. But who could convince the Parliament to do anything for lowly tax collectors?

Tom's debates at the White Hart Inn had shown him how to make a good argument. And his work with the Society of Twelve had taught him about politics.

Surely he could show Parliament that it didn't make sense to pay the excisemen so poorly. Tom told his ideas to other excisemen and found that his words inspired them. They agreed that Tom should speak for them all.

Tom wrote a pamphlet called *The Case of the Officers of Excise*. In the pamphlet, he argued that it was not only unjust to pay hardworking excisemen so poorly, it was just plain stupid. How did Parliament ever expect to hire honest, intelligent men if they didn't pay their tax collectors fairly? Who could blame a man for taking a bribe now and then if that was the only way to put food on the table? Tom asked other excisemen to sign a petition supporting his argument. He also asked them to help pay for printing costs. Nearly all of the three thousand excisemen donated money. Even so, Tom had to pay for most of the printing costs himself.

In the winter of 1772, he arrived in London with four thousand copies of the pamphlet and a lot of hope. He handed out his pamphlets to members of Parliament and some other important people. He pleaded his case to whomever would listen. But it did no good. Tom had inspired thousands of excisemen to believe that they had a right to better wages. But he could not convince Parliament to change a thing.

The lawmakers refused to pass a law that would increase wages. It seemed that all the logic in the world was powerless against the ultimate power of Parliament and the king.

Tom returned to Lewes a disappointed man. Soon after that, he lost a lot more than his optimism. In April 1774, he lost his job as an exciseman. This time the Board of Excise Commissioners charged him with leaving his post without permission. The board said Tom should have been working in Lewes rather than spending time in London. This reasoning seemed like an excuse to get rid of a troublemaker. But Tom could do nothing about it.

Without money from his job, Tom went bankrupt. Once again he was forced to sell off nearly everything he owned. At the age of thirty-seven, he had nothing. The situation was too much for Elizabeth. Since their marriage, she and Tom had fought often. After some discussion, they agreed to separate from each other that summer and go their own ways. It was an unusual arrangement, but it seemed to be the only solution. Tom decided to leave Lewes and return to London. Maybe something good would be waiting for him there.

4

A Fresh Start

Tom walked through the streets of London, taking in the city's sights, sounds, and smells. He went to his favorite coffeehouses and bookshops, attended lectures, and spent time with old friends. The bustling streets and his London friends reminded him that life was worth living. It made Tom think about turning his life around—maybe even seeking adventure. He no longer wanted to be a sailor, but he still had an interest in going to the American colonies. He could start a fresh new life there.

Tom had learned from a friend that a famous ambassador from Philadelphia, Pennsylvania, was in

London. Benjamin Franklin often came to Britain's capital on behalf of the American colonists. He had helped convince Great Britain to put a stop to certain taxes that the colonists believed were unfair. But Parliament refused to change a tax on the colonists' favorite drink, tea. Even worse, in 1773 Britain had passed the hated Tea Act. This law heavily favored the East India Company, a British tea seller. The law all but forced colonists to buy their tea from this one British source. In response, many outraged colonists avoided buying tea altogether.

On December 16, 1773, a group of angry colonists in Boston, Massachusetts, went much further. That evening they attacked three ships full of British tea and dumped all the tea into Boston Harbor. King George punished Boston by closing down its port so no goods could enter or leave the harbor. Colonial merchants who relied on Boston's busy port could no longer sell their products overseas. Needed foreign products would not be allowed into the colonies through Boston either. King George refused to open the port again until colonists agreed to pay for the lost tea. In the meantime, he sent thousands of British soldiers to Massachusetts to patrol the streets of Boston. Matters were only getting worse. Franklin hoped to ease tensions between Britain and the colonies.

Tom was able to meet with the American ambassador. Franklin encouraged him to go to Pennsylvania. He even wrote Tom a letter of recommendation that would help him find a job in Philadelphia.

By the end of September, Tom had packed his few belongings, gathered together what little money he had, and purchased a ticket to Philadelphia. The journey on the *London Packet* was miserable. The seas were rough, and a disease known as ship fever spread to nearly all the passengers. When he arrived in Philadelphia on November 30, Tom was too sick to pay much attention to the city. Instead, he spent six weeks with relatives of the ship's captain, recovering in bed.

When he finally regained his health in early January 1775, Tom explored the streets of Philadelphia. In some ways, the city was like a miniature London. With about 30,000 citizens, it was the largest city in all the thirteen colonies. It was a center of business and trade. The city had recently become a political center as well. The First Continental Congress had just finished meeting in Philadelphia to discuss growing tensions between the colonies and Britain. The meeting had gathered together representatives from nearly all the colonies.

The American colonies were an ocean away from Britain. But Tom observed that the colonists considered themselves to be as British as anyone living in England. Yet Tom felt that there was something refreshingly different about the American colonists. They were self-reliant, independent people. Tom was struck by the positive, confident, and friendly attitude of the people he met.

Tom quickly found a room to rent in the center of the city on the corner of Market and Front Streets. He was within walking distance of a library, a coffeehouse, several taverns, and a good bookshop. He spent many hours in that bookshop and gradually came to know its owner, Robert Aitken.

Aitken owned a printing press and was planning to publish a new monthly magazine. Aitken wanted his magazine to be something like Britain's *Gentleman's Magazine,* which included news, poems, and stories. Families in the colonies subscribed to this magazine, but it wasn't written for them. Aitken wanted to publish a monthly magazine specifically written for the colonists.

Tom listened to Aitken's plan with great interest, especially when the man asked him if he might like to write for the magazine. Tom agreed to write an introduction for the first issue.

After reading it, Robert Aitken offered Tom the job of editor. He needed him to start right away. The first issue of the *Pennsylvania Magazine* was to come out later that month. That didn't leave them much time.

The *Pennsylvania Magazine* was fifty-two pages sewn together between two blue paper covers. When it came out on January 24, 1775, hundreds of colonists purchased the magazine. By then Tom was already thinking of new ideas for the next issue.

For the first time in his life, Tom had a job that he felt passionate about. Here was a chance to educate average people the way Benjamin Martin and James Ferguson had educated the general public in London. Tom took care to write his articles in the same way that he debated. He made the subjects of science and politics understandable to common people.

While winter melted into spring, Tom stayed busy writing and collecting work by other writers. He filled the magazine with news, poetry, essays from abroad, and articles on science, politics, and religion. He also expressed many of his own opinions about how life should be. He used a common practice of signing his articles with made-up names, such as "Atlanticus" and "Justice and Humanity." The names reflected the ideas and values he promoted in his articles.

In one article, Tom condemned duels. He believed there were better ways for two grown men to solve a disagreement than to battle to the death with guns or swords. In another article, he argued against treating animals cruelly. He even attacked the colonists for their "monstrous" practice of owning other human beings. In doing so, he became one of very few people in the colonies to speak out publicly against slavery. Slavery was legal in all thirteen colonies, so it was a touchy subject. But Tom felt it was wrong.

Slavery wasn't the only touchy subject in the colonies. Many colonists were still angry with the king and Parliament. Great Britain continued to assert its right to tax the colonies. And British soldiers continued to watch over the colonists to make sure they did not cause any more trouble. Anyone who spoke out in public against the king or organized anti-British meetings could be punished for the serious crime of treason (betrayal of the king).

Robert Aitken wanted to be sure his *Pennsylvania Magazine* steered clear of anything to do with Great Britain or taxes. For his part, Tom had little to say on the subject. There were plenty of other things to write about. The magazine had become extremely popular in the colonies. Tom was building a reputation for himself as a man with a powerful pen.

5

Facts, Arguments, and *Common Sense*

Tom could hardly believe his ears as he listened to the talk at a town meeting. Concerned citizens had gathered together to learn about a recent fight between British soldiers and colonists in Massachusetts. On the morning of April 19, 1775, British troops had attacked the towns of Lexington and Concord. Their goal had been to seize weapons and supplies from anti-British colonists. But they ended up opening fire on a group of colonial militiamen. Both colonists and British soldiers died fighting.

The more he learned, the more Tom's blood boiled. Taxes were one thing. But killing one's own people?

Tom couldn't believe that Britain had allowed that to happen. Someone had to speak out against the violence, even if he might be accused of treason.

Tom began writing pieces that criticized Britain and upheld the American colonies as a land of bounty and liberty. He pointed out that power in the British government was reserved for the wealthy. Power was passed down from son to son within the same families. King George himself had been born into his power. Tom argued that the king had not earned power by proving himself to be good leader. Therefore, he should not be followed without question. If a king refused to treat his people fairly, Tom wrote, then the people had the right to take action. In Tom's view, Britain was giving the colonists no choice but to fight for their independence.

Many people read Tom's writings, but not everyone agreed with them. Although the king had made quite a few enemies in the colonies, many colonists were still loyal to him. These loyalists were outraged by Tom's fiery opinions.

Even some who were not so loyal to the king were uncomfortable with Tom's ideas. For many colonists, the attacks at Lexington and Concord had been quickly forgotten. Surely one battle wasn't worth breaking away from Great Britain, the mother country.

How could the colonies fend for themselves without Britain's help? No, it was better to keep quiet and try to solve problems peacefully.

But the battles of Lexington and Concord had marked the beginning of a war between Britain and the colonies. Only a handful of people, Tom included, understood that there was no turning back.

The cause of American freedom had ignited a fire inside Tom. He felt sure that a free America could be different from any other nation in the world. America, Tom thought, was destined to be the world's first democratic republic. He pictured it as a country where citizens had the right to choose their own leaders and lawmakers. There would be no king or queen. There would be no Parliament full of wealthy men that few people had elected. An American government would be by and for the people.

Tom was not alone in his beliefs. A growing number of colonists, known as patriots, argued that the time had come for independence. Outspoken leaders such as Patrick Henry in Virginia, Benjamin Rush in Philadelphia, and Samuel Adams in Boston were sounding the call for freedom. They believed that an independent America held great promise for its people. And they believed that war was the only way to achieve independence.

But the Americans would have to win the war against Britain. The Continental Congress had recently chosen George Washington to lead the colonies' Continental Army. General Washington was an excellent military leader. But even the greatest leader couldn't win a war without soldiers. And the colonies were sorely lacking in soldiers. Few people wanted anything to do with the war. After all, they thought, who in their right mind would sign up to fight against the best army in the world? A ragtag team of militiamen wouldn't stand a chance against Great Britain's red-coated army.

Someone needed to convince the colonists that American liberty was not only possible but worth dying for. To many supporters of the war, it seemed clear that Thomas Paine was that someone. His attacks on Britain were becoming more and more convincing.

At this time, the best way to reach many people at once was to publish a pamphlet. Pamphlets could be printed cheaply and sold cheaply to hundreds of people. It was one of the fastest ways to broadcast an argument and to convince people of a certain opinion. The patriot Benjamin Rush asked Tom to write a pamphlet that would inspire the colonists to get behind the war.

Tom knew that it would be dangerous to publicly call for war. But he was willing to take the risk. Nothing had ever inspired him like this. Tom had a once-in-a-lifetime chance to change the world—and he was going to take it.

Throughout the fall and early winter, Tom worked intently on his pamphlet. He struggled with his sentences, trying to find the best way to express himself. Whenever he finished a new passage of his essay, he came knocking on Benjamin Rush's door. He read aloud what he had written and made changes based on the patriot's comments.

He finished the manuscript in early December 1775. Just to make sure it was good enough, he showed it to several more people. One of those people was Benjamin Franklin, who was back in Philadelphia. Franklin and other patriots strongly approved of Tom's arguments for war.

Tom tried to think of a good title for his pamphlet. It had to be a title that would get people to pick it up and read it. Benjamin Rush suggested that Tom call his pamphlet *Common Sense*, because, he said, that was exactly what it contained.

In *Common Sense*, Tom argued that it was ridiculous to obey a ruler who was simply born into power. And it was equally wrongheaded to believe that the colonists needed Great Britain to survive. The colonies were no longer like helpless children. They had grown up, and it was about time they took charge of themselves. If the colonies won independence, America would be the first truly free nation in the world. But if the colonists remained chained to British rule, they would always be powerless. "The sun never shined on a cause of greater worth," Tom wrote. With a cause so worthy, how could the colonists lose?

Common Sense went on sale January 10, 1776. Colonists snatched it up almost as soon as it was printed. Booksellers could barely keep up with the demand. Within two weeks, the pamphlet had to be reprinted. After that, it was reprinted time and time again. It quickly became the best-selling pamphlet in the colonies, with at least 150,000 copies in print.

Thousands of colonists read or heard Tom's arguments for war. The result was explosive. While some colonists had discussed such radical ideas privately, Thomas Paine seemed to be shouting them from the rooftops. No one had so publicly or strongly argued for freedom from Britain. And no one had done so in such plain language. The pamphlet was written especially for ordinary people. That was important because farmers and other workers would be needed as soldiers.

Not everyone liked what Tom had to say, but few could ignore his words. He indeed inspired some men to join the Continental Army and fight for the cause of liberty. Others were so angered by Thomas Paine that they wrote nasty articles attacking him.

Tom was as pleased by the positive reaction to his pamphlet as he was angered by the criticism. He had no problem attacking the king, whom he called "the Royal Brute of Britain." But he was extremely sensitive to other people's attacks on him. Still, he continued to believe passionately in the cause of American independence. He felt that war was the only way to gain that independence, and he was determined to do whatever he could to help lead the Americans to victory.

6

Crisis in America

While colonists debated the ideas in *Common Sense,* the Continental Congress decided it was time for some strong words of its own. They asked Thomas Jefferson, a lawmaker from Virginia, to draft the Declaration of Independence. This document stated that the American colonies had a right to be an independent nation. Congress adopted the Declaration on July 4, 1776, and it was signed by fifty-six members.

Meanwhile thousands of copies of *Common Sense* continued to sell. Tom made very little money from these sales. What he did earn, he gave to the army. The soldiers were in desperate need of supplies.

Tom found new ways to help the Americans. In the fall of 1776, he worked as an aide to General Nathanael Greene. Tom spent the next two months with the general and his troops. He also watched more and more British soldiers flood onto America's shores. The huge British army was just too daunting for many American soldiers. Some Americans deserted, or fled the army. Many of those who stuck it out had serious doubts about whether they could possibly win any battles against Great Britain's powerful military.

Tom passed around copies of *Common Sense* to the soldiers and did his best to lift their spirits. At the same time, he worried about how the rest of the colonists might be feeling about the war. If no one believed the Americans could beat the British, they would lose the war for sure.

Tom began to write war reports for a newspaper called the *Pennsylvania Journal*. He hoped to be the public's eyes and ears. He wanted to tell the truth about the war's progress, but he also wanted to keep the colonists' spirits high. Americans throughout the colonies were terrified that Washington's army would not be able to protect them. They feared that their town or city would be invaded by the British. What would happen then?

Tom tried his best to calm people's nerves with his carefully worded accounts of the war. But he saw that something more was needed. Winter was coming, and General Washington struggled to keep his army from falling apart. The American troops were under-fed and underclothed. They were hungry, cold, and hopeless. Many of them had volunteered to be sol-diers only for a few months. They were eager to get back to their families, shops, and farms. The time had come for another pamphlet.

In December 1776, Tom left the army. He braved the cold weather to walk the thirty-five miles back to Philadelphia. His plan was to publish a new pamphlet there.

When he arrived in the city, he was shocked by what he saw. People were fleeing Philadelphia, which had become America's capital. The people there had heard that the British army was preparing to take over the capital. They seemed convinced that the American army was no match for the red-coated soldiers.

To Tom, this behavior was truly disgraceful. How dare the Americans doubt their own soldiers. Didn't they realize the cause of American independence was great enough to overcome any army? Tom desperately needed to find a way to inspire the people of Philadelphia and, most important, Washington's army.

Otherwise, the British just might take over the city. That would be a terrible blow. Tom decided to call his next pamphlet *The American Crisis.* It would be more fiery than *Common Sense.*

"These are the times that try men's souls," Tom wrote. Many a person might "shrink from the service of their country; but he that stands it now deserves the love and thanks of man and woman." Times were hard, Tom knew, and it was tempting to give up. But those who stuck with this war for independence would go down in history as heroes.

The American Crisis was published in December 1776. When General Washington read Thomas Paine's words, he ordered that the pamphlet be read to every single soldier. On Christmas Day 1776, soldiers all across the colonies listened to Thomas Paine's inspiring words. The pamphlet reminded the soldiers why they were fighting. It reminded them that they were not losers but heroes.

After hearing *The American Crisis,* many soldiers were willing to stay and fight. And, against the odds, the Americans won their next battle at Trenton, New Jersey. This prevented the British from advancing farther toward Philadelphia.

Tom's plan was to write thirteen parts to *The American Crisis,* one for each colony. He would write a new installment whenever he thought the public needed encouragement. Unfortunately, *The American Crisis* did not earn Tom any money. In fact, he spent his own money to get it printed. He needed some way to earn a living because he was no longer assisting the army. To his relief, the Continental Congress took notice of the fiery Englishman who had written patriotic pamphlets.

In April 1777, the congress appointed Tom secretary to the Committee for Foreign Affairs. The congress had formed this committee to build relationships with friendly countries in Europe, especially France. Committee members hoped to convince foreign countries to donate money and supplies to the American army. As secretary, Tom took notes at meetings, wrote letters for committee members, and kept track of important papers. He was proud of his new job. It proved to him that the Americans respected him for all he had done in the name of American liberty.

Tom's new job kept him busy—so busy he didn't have much time to write. But by that summer, he had plenty to say. British troops still greatly outnumbered Washington's struggling army. The American general had not been able to prevent the British from coming ever closer to Philadelphia. Citizens of the capital feared a British attack. Once again, people were fleeing the city. Tom sat down to write a new installment of *The American Crisis*. He called on Americans to stand behind their army, and he urged them to help "set a country free."

His words fell on deaf ears. Most Philadelphians had no time to read a new pamphlet. They were too busy running for their lives. In the middle of the night on September 19, 1777, bells rang out to alert Philadelphians that the British were coming. Tom stepped outside to see the moonlit streets filled with panicked men, women, and children rushing out of the city. Even the congress made hasty plans to move its headquarters. Tom wanted to stay in Philadelphia, but he knew that he'd be killed if the British caught him. In the end, he fled, too.

7

The Greatest Revolution

The war was looking grim for the Americans. Britain always seemed to have the upper hand. The Continental Army still lacked basic war supplies, food, and clothing. Some people grumbled about Washington. They questioned his ability to lead America to victory. But Tom had great faith in the general. He wrote another installment to *The American Crisis* to lift people's spirits and calm their nerves.

Tom wrote this latest pamphlet while staying with an acquaintance. In the months since he had escaped Philadelphia, he'd had no place to call home. He had stayed in the homes of various friends, and he had visited army camps to keep tabs on the war. At one point, he even visited the Continental Army's main camp at Valley Forge, Pennsylvania, and talked with General Washington. His whole life seemed to be taken up with the cause of American liberty.

Eventually, Tom returned to his work as secretary for the Committee for Foreign Affairs. In December 1778, he became caught in a bitter fight among members of the congress. They were trying to decide what to do about a man named Silas Deane. Deane had been trying to convince France to give the Americans more money for the war. Some members of the congress believed he had kept some of the money for himself. Tom had seen papers that seemed to prove Deane was guilty.

Silas Deane had many loyal friends who defended him. Other men were convinced that he had done something terribly wrong. Although it was none of his business, Tom jumped right into the middle of the argument. He couldn't understand how the man could use the cause of liberty to make money for himself. Tom was disgusted, and he wasn't afraid to say so. To him, Deane was a traitor to the cause of the American Revolution. Tom published an article attacking Deane for his actions. To his surprise, supporters of Deane's accused Tom of being an enemy of the revolution. It was a criticism that must have stung.

In January 1779, Tom lost his job as secretary for the Committee for Foreign Affairs. This was the second time in his life that he'd lost a job for speaking his mind. He'd also been fired by the Board of Excise Commissioners for trying to get better wages. He seemed to have a knack for getting himself in trouble.

The next few months were rough ones for Tom. People attacked him in articles and in person. Men shouted at him on the street. Once he was physically attacked by three men who called him a traitor. Even some of his own friends turned on him. He began to feel that he was no longer welcome in America.

Tom had never been much good at taking criticism. He just wanted to hide, but his friends wouldn't let him. The many people who remembered Thomas Paine's contributions to America came to his defense. They wrote articles to fend off the negative attacks against him. They organized public rallies in support of him. And they fought back against those who tried to destroy his reputation. They reminded people that Thomas Paine had inspired hundreds of men to fight for American liberty. He had stood behind the war when others wanted to give up. The passionate support of Tom's friends and admirers worked. His harshest critics stopped attacking him. Tom felt he could show his face in public again.

Tom went back to writing pamphlets, but his words were less and less needed as the war went on. Things had begun to turn around for the colonists. To the astonishment of the world, the Americans were beating back the British. An American victory seemed within reach. Finally, the last major battle of the war was fought at Yorktown, where American forces crushed the British in 1781. Still, the fighting went on for two more years.

In 1783 even Britain came to realize that it could no longer fight against the proud patriots. That spring, the Americans and the British signed a peace treaty. The United States of America was officially free from British rule.

To celebrate the Americans' success, Tom wrote a final pamphlet, *The Last Crisis*. " 'The times that tried men's souls' are over," he wrote. He called the American victory "the greatest and completest revolution the world ever knew."

After the war, some Americans wanted to repay Thomas Paine for his hard work and his commitment to the cause of liberty. One of those Americans was George Washington. He convinced the country to reward Tom with some land. The state of New York offered Tom a home in New Rochelle, New York. Tom also received a grant of more than three thousand dollars.

Tom settled into his house in New Rochelle and tried his best to enjoy a quiet life there. But he was not made for a quiet life. His years as a staymaker had taught him that. By 1787 he had decided to leave America for Europe. As Tom prepared to set sail for France, his mind filled with revolutionary ideas for the future.

Afterword

In Europe, Thomas Paine's thoughts turned from politics to his old love of science. He had become fascinated by the idea of designing a modern bridge. But he soon got caught up in politics again. Just as the American colonists had done, the people of France were beginning to question their king, Louis XVI. In 1789 a bloody revolution broke out.

Tom supported the French Revolution. He still passionately believed in the people's right to choose their own leaders and governments. In 1791 and 1792, he wrote *The Rights of Man* in defense of the ideas behind the French Revolution. Like *Common Sense,* this publication became a best-seller that influenced thousands of people.

Although Tom supported the cause of French liberty, he spoke out against some of his fellow revolutionaries. A group of rebels wanted to execute France's king, Louis XVI. Eventually, that group gained power in France, beheaded the king, and imprisoned or killed those who had publicly disagreed with them. Tom ended up in jail at the end of 1793. During his ten months of imprisonment, he wrote the first part of a book called *The Age of Reason.* In it he criticized religions that discouraged free thought by expecting people to follow their rules and customs without question. The book shocked and angered some people and inspired others. It quickly became another best-seller.

In 1794 the American government saved Tom from being put to death in France. It offered him American citizenship and ordered his release from prison. Yet Tom's final years in the United States were difficult ones. The unusual ideas he promoted in *The Age of Reason* had made him an outcast. Thomas Paine died in New York on June 8, 1809, a forgotten hero.

Time and time again, Thomas Paine had risked his reputation, well-being—even his life—to stand up for his beliefs. From his fight for British exciseman to his defense of just governments and free thought, Thomas Paine had devoted himself to the cause of liberty. His fiery words had made complicated arguments convincing and clear. In all his writings, he had strived to offer "nothing more than simple facts, plain arguments, and common sense."

Selected Bibliography

Ayer, A. J. *Thomas Paine*. New York: Atheneum, 1988.

Bailyn, Bernard. *Faces of Revolution: Personalities and Themes in the Struggle for American Independence*. New York: Alfred A. Knoff, 1990.

Flemming, Thomas. *Liberty! The American Revolution*. New York: Viking, 1997.

Fruchtman, Jack Jr. *Thomas Paine: Apostle of Freedom*. New York: Four Walls Eight Windows, 1994.

Keane, John. *Tom Paine: A Political Life*. Boston: Little Brown and Company, 1995.

Meltzer, Milton. *Tom Paine: Voice of Revolution*. New York: Franklin Watts, 1996.

Meyeroff, Stephen. *The Call for Independence: The Story of the American Revolution and Its Causes*. Cherry Hill, NJ: Oak Tree Publishers, 1996.

Middlekauff, Robert. *The Glorious Cause: The American Revolution, 1763–1789*. New York: Oxford University Press, 1982.

Paine, Thomas. *The Life and Works of Thomas Paine*. Willam M. der Weyde, ed. New Rochelle, NY: Thomas Paine National Historical Association, 1925.

Wood, Gordon S. *The Radicalism of the American Revolution*. New York: Vintage Books, 1991.

Index